COLOR ME SEATTLE

The Official Coloring Book of the Puget Sound Region

Illustrated by
Kristine DeLong

Published by

EMERALD POINT PRESS®
SEATTLE, WASHINGTON

ISBN 0-9637816-4-2
Printed in Hong Kong

CITYSCAPE

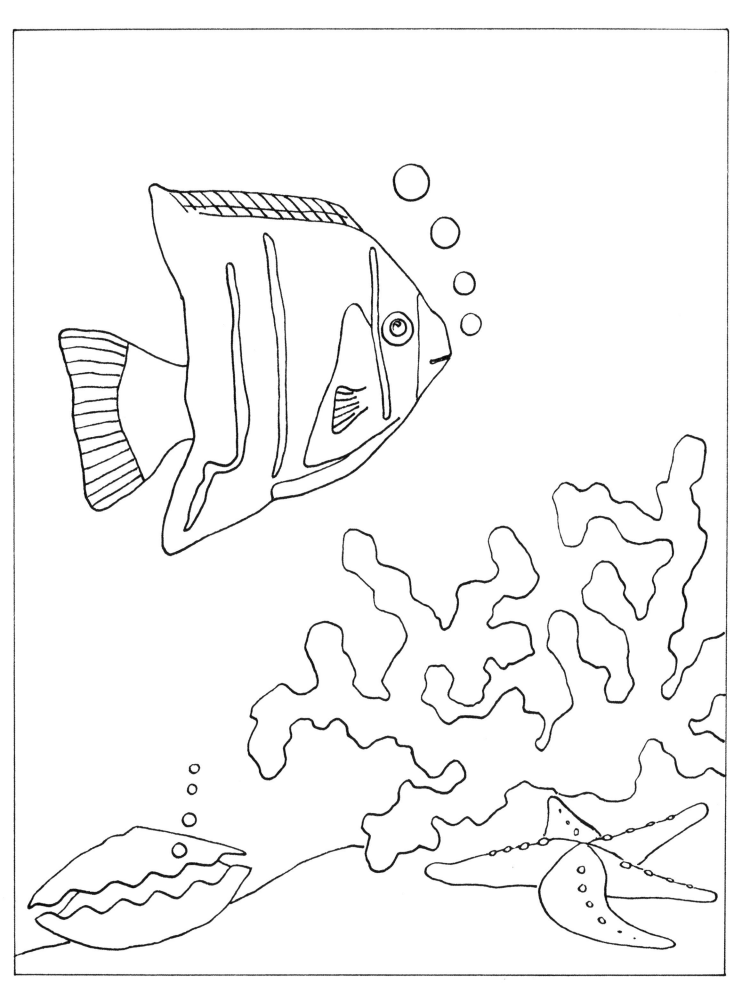

AQUARIUM

LIGHTHOUSE

SNOQUALMIE FALLS 5

6   **MOUNT RAINIER**

FISH LADDER

INTERNATIONAL DISTRICT

LION - WOODLAND PARK ZOO

10   **FLOATPLANE**

TOUR BOAT

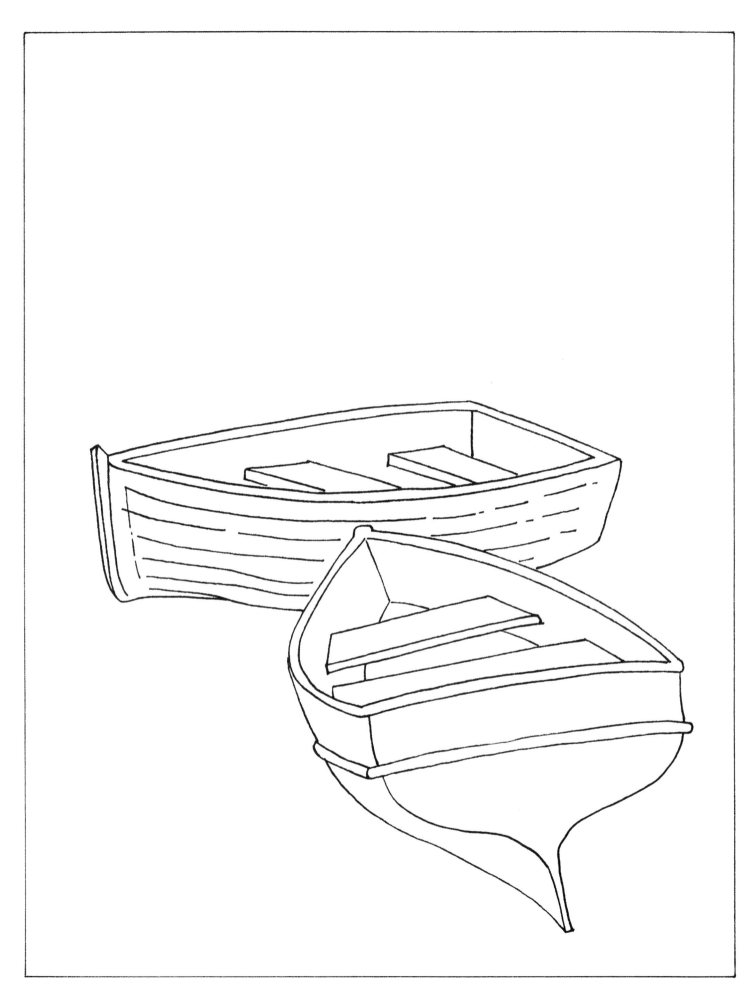

WOODEN BOATS

SMITH TOWER BUILDING

FIREBOAT

BALD EAGLE 15

OLYMPIC MOUNTAINS AND PUGET SOUND

DRAWBRIDGE

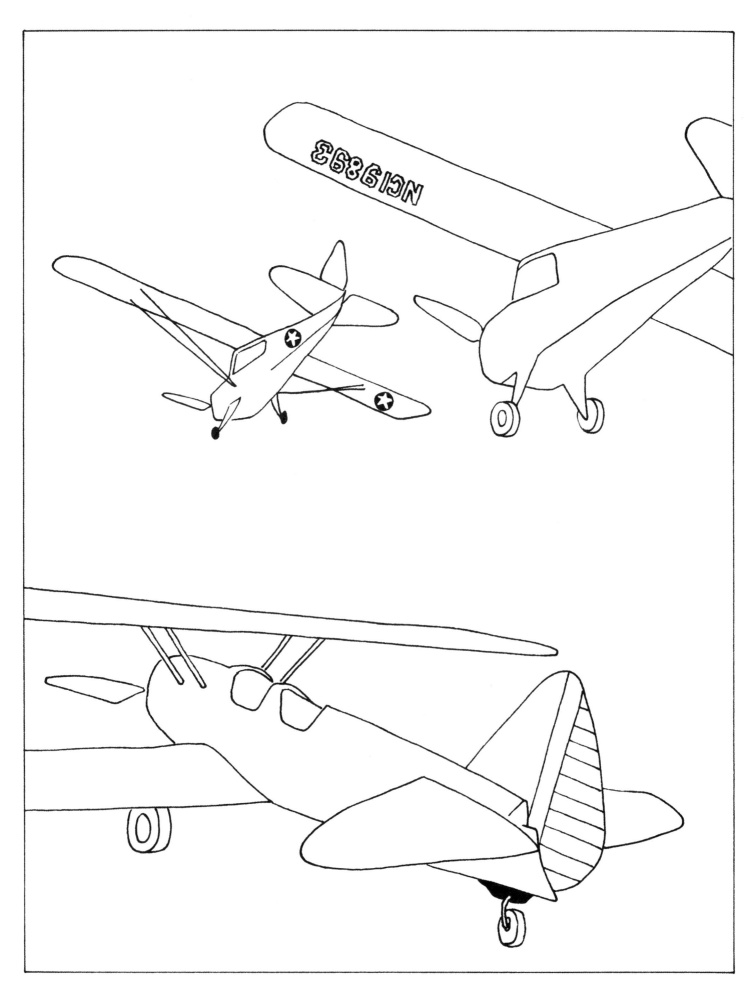

MUSEUM OF FLIGHT

SPACE NEEDLE 19

PIKE PLACE MARKET

PIKE PLACE MARKET

ORCA

PUGET SOUND FERRY

TOTEM POLE

HOUSEBOAT 25

FISHING BOAT

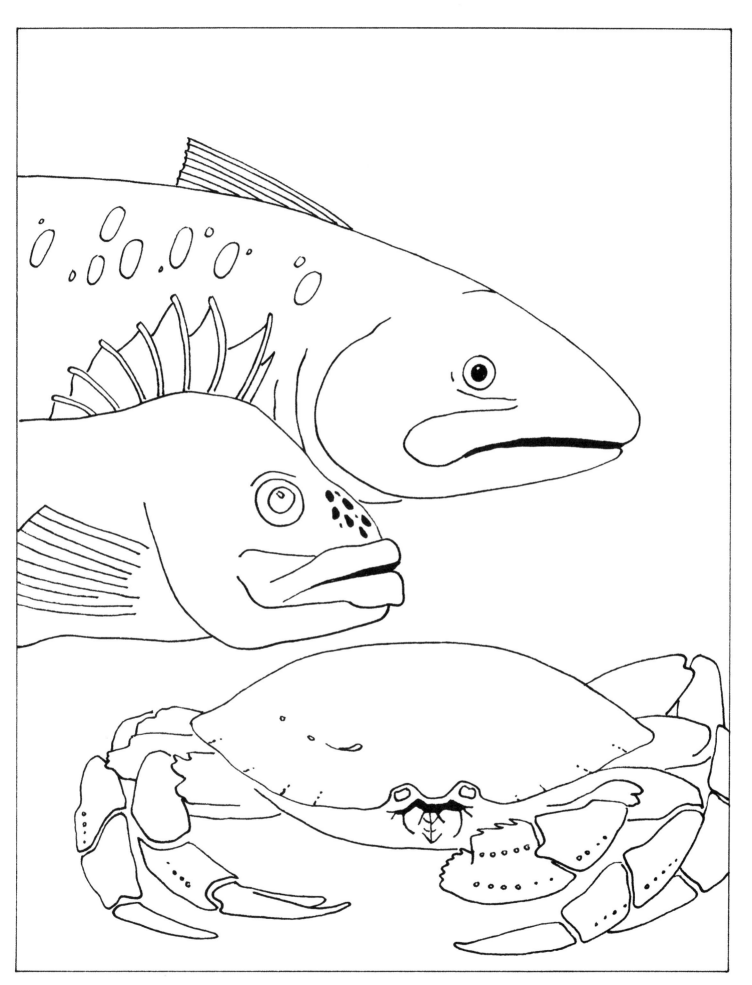

CRAB AND FISH 27

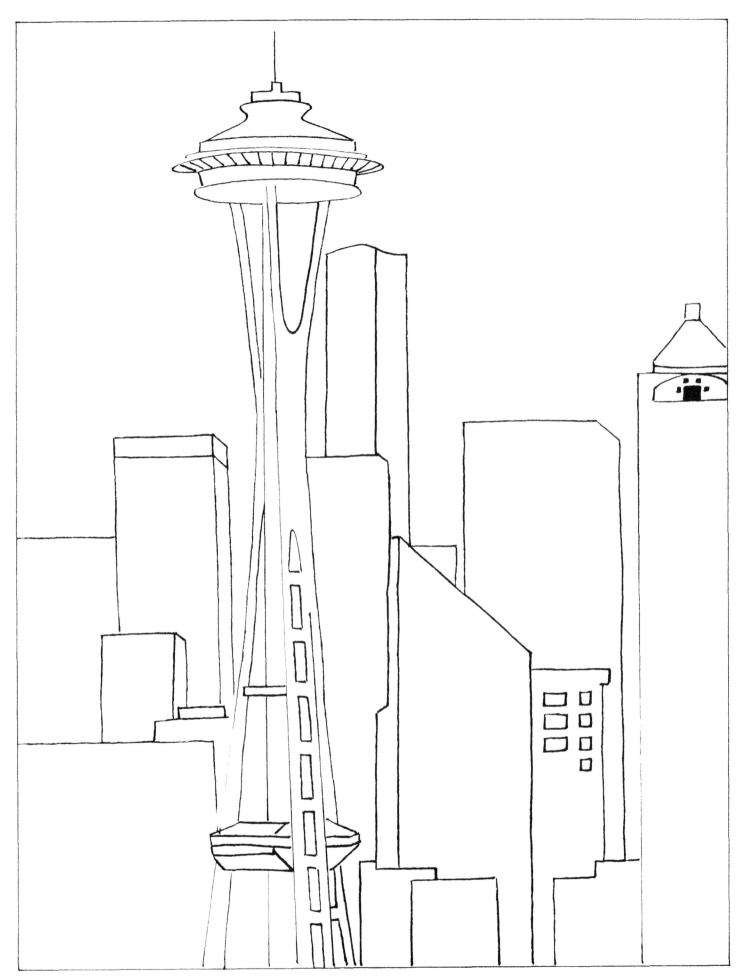

SPACE NEEDLE - CITY SKYLINE

RAIN OR SHINE - SEATTLE IS FINE

KUBOTA GARDENS

FLOATING BRIDGE 31

WATERFRONT STREETCAR

COFFEE DRINKS

MONORAIL

SEAGULL

TUGBOAT

PIONEER SQUARE

VICTORIAN HOUSE

ELEPHANT - WOODLAND PARK ZOO

39

TULIPS